I am Hope

How I Overcame
Physical and Sexual Abuse

Hope Champaigne

LOVEHOPE BOOKS

Acknowledgements

First, I want to thank God for my testimony. My story is one of heartache but also joy; I've learned Psalm 30:5b "weeping may endure for a night but joy comes in the morning." God has purposed me for such a time as this because *He was wounded for my transgression, bruised for my iniquities, the chastisement of my peace was upon him and with His stripes I am healed (Isaiah 53:5 emphasis added)*. For I know I am *"fearfully and wonderfully made"* (Ps. 139:13-14). There is no secret what the Lord can do, as I know personally, what He did for me.

Next, I want to thank my family, friends, and strangers whom I shared my testimony for encouraging me to write my story. To my children: Iree, Raheen, and Dana Jr., I am so proud to be your mom. To my grandson Joshua, words cannot express the joy and love I have for you. I hope this book will be a testimony to you all as you work to fulfill your destiny.

To my siblings, Rico, Richard, and Nicole, we

shared our mother's womb; I love you much! To my adopted siblings, Cedric, Cedra, and CJ, and to my God-sister Suni, I love you all.

Special thanks to my aunt Colette Champaigne for always understanding who I am and pushing me to be the best me I can be. Thanks for all the talks, calls, and tears we have shed together throughout the years.

Thanks also to my aunts, Marva (who is waiting for me in heaven), Gloria, Dorothy, Willamae, Mary (Eunice), Paulette (Mona), Gwendolyn, Christina (Grelynn). Special shout out to the most loving men to me, my uncles, Anthony (Tug), Curtis, Bruce, and Elliot (who is RIP).To my grandfather Herman who always accepted and supported me. I love you more than words can describe. Hugs and kisses to all of my nieces and nephews. You are the reason I am the woman I am today.

A special acknowledgement goes to my beautiful and courageous grandmother, Martha Champaigne, for teaching me first how to pray and the power of singing spiritual songs. You taught me to worship God and I am eternally grateful. I love you much.

There are several others. I must thank. Valerie and Felicia, for opening your doors and being surrogate moms to me. You taught me to keep my head up and look good doing so.

To my Godmother Deborah, thank you for giving me such a powerful and strong name.

Finally, yet importantly, I want to thank all of my friends who have prayed, cried, and encouraged me through this journey: Monique, for more than 20 years of friendship. To my brothers and sister in the faith: Margo, Janice, Nickela, Courtney, CJ, Melanie, and Kiki-no words can express the love and respect I have for each of you.

To special cousins, Ebony and Marlo, I am so grateful for the relationship we have. We are more like siblings than first cousins.

Special recognition to Latoya Williams, thank you for reading my story and contributing your thoughts.

FOREWORD

I have known Hope Coleman for more than sixteen years and as I read this book, the word that comes to mind is courage. It takes courage to be transparent and vulnerable to public opinion. Hope is a brave woman for writing her story, revealing so much of her life for the world to see.

I read her BIO recently and one of the most powerful statements she says is that "Shame is no longer apart of her biography. She believes that God's grace has delivered her and by writing this book, she is extending His grace to the nations. Even though Hope describes details of her abuse and provides snippets of her life, the message she expresses the most is her faith in God.

I met Hope when she joined a church I was pasturing. As a Licensed Professional Counselor, I have seen the kind of abuse Hope describes and she suffered. She shared the unworthiness she felt answering the call of God on her life. At one time, she expressed how devalued she felt as a Christian. I became her Pastor and spiritual advisor at that time she needed direction and encouragement; that is how God allowed our paths to cross. My wife Anna and I have watched Hope grow into a mature Christian. She overcame the darkness of her path and now walks in the light of our Savior Jesus Christ.

Everyone has some hidden something that is impossible to overcome all on their own but with God's help, deliverance is their blessed assurance. They too can learn as Hope has, to rely upon Him and His Spirit for guidance to living life in victory.

Hope Coleman has the courage to share her testimony in the awaiting pages and shares the hope of Christ. God met her where she was, healed, delivered, and set her free from her past.

I believe that Hope's story is not only powerful but one that will help others whose been living with the shame of childhood abuse. My wife and I are proud of her accomplishments and happy to consider her a part of our extended family.

Dr. Juenarrl Keith, D.MIN, LPC
Presiding Elder of the Mount Pleasant District

Preface

For You formed my inward parts; You covered me in my mother's womb. I will praise You, for I am fearfully and wonderfully made
(Ps 139:13-14a)

The above scripture is the mantra of my life's story. I have a testimony and it is time to tell it to the world. For a significant time in my life, I did not feel valued as a human being. As a child, there were toxic words spoken to me. I felt I had no identity so I believed those words. I did not know Jesus or what He had completed on the cross. I did not learn His love until the day I accepted Him and He entered my heart.

I was told that I would not amount to anything. I was a child and it was hard to hear those words by the one person who is supposed to love me. Those words left me feeling worthless and hopeless. I believed nothing in life could be good. If all there was to life was being put down, slapped, punched, and beaten all because I woke up, then, what was the reason to keep on living?

I was given the name Hope, but that is all it was, a name. Who was the person? What was my identity? Who was Hope? My Godmother gave me the name Hope for a reason, but not even, she knew at the time how meaningful my name would become. My Godmother and I came to know the significance of my name. My name was ordained and appointed by God. He foreknew I would need hope to survive. My name serves as a constant reminder of the goodness of the Lord.

From the time I was about five years of age I wondered who I was and why was I stuck in this life? What did I do to deserve this hard time called life? From that young age, I knew something was not right. But then again what was love? I did not know love or could comprehend it. I did not know God or that he truly existed. All I knew is that my name was Hope and love was being bruised black and blue, inside and out.

Pain was my best friend and for a long time I could not terminate the relationship between us. She traveled everywhere with me. I carried her around like luggage; the only problem, I didn't unpack. I carried the same baggage around for years until an angel gave me a new set of luggage in the personhood of Christ.

I was born to a teenage mom in 1973 and a father who was not around at the time. My grandmother describes me as a beautiful bright-skinned baby whom she believe is gifted. She believes God has His hands upon my life. As her first-born grandchild, she may be a little bit biased. Nevertheless, in my mind I believe that I am her favorite granddaughter.

I may not have had the love of a mother, but the love of a grandmother and aunts gave me hope. There is no way for me to compare since I did not feel love from my parents. A mother is supposed to be a nurturer, be loving and protective. I was not blessed with that mother. I learned firsthand, some women who are blessed to have children do not always have that natural "mothering instinct."

Physical and sexual abuse are not overrated, it is understated. The shame that comes with abuse can place a person on a very destructive path. Its effects can last for many, many years. It has taken its toll on my life, but I am still here pressing toward the mark of the higher calling. It took me some time to accept Christ's unconditional love for me, to fully surrender my life to him, learn the power of forgiveness, and become equipped in walking in love with people.

It is not always easy, everyday it is a challenge, but with God's help, all things are possible if we believe in Christ. Every day we must cast all our cares upon Him, knowing that He cares for us. Only God loves us best. I am reminded daily as I wash the dishes that during my times of trouble, I saw only one footprint in the sand; it was **God** carrying me through.

I pray this book will be a blessing to you and it encourages you to one day tell your story.

Table of Contents

CHAPTER ONE

Hallelujah is a word I can now say with the peace and joy of God in my heart. For a longtime, I did not know what it really meant to live. I did not know love or what it felt like to be loved because of my abusive childhood.

I was born on March 24. I share this wonderful birthdate with my father. As a child, I learned that I did not matter. I was about four years of age when the verbal abuse started. I was about five years old when she started beating me.

I lived in constant fear and anxiety of my mother. The first thing she said, I am not able to forget is that she did not like "foxtails". I asked her what that was and she expressed she did not like "little girls". Girls were too much trouble.

I was about five years old when she told me I would not amount to anything but a prostitute. I felt worthless. Who coined the term, "sticks and stones may break my bones but words will never hurt me?" It is a lie from the pit of hell. Words do hurt and they stick with you for a long time.

Words almost destroyed my life. I wanted to commit suicide because of the negative things spoken to me as a child. I am a product of verbal, physical, and sexual abuse. I spent years of my life in darkness, with no hope, dysfunctional love, and no need of God. Or so I thought…

I did not know if God loved me. Why did He give me an awful life? Why was my mother so hateful towards me? Why did my father neglect me? Why did my close relative touch me? I never said I hated God, but I did not say I loved Him either. I felt this way mainly because I did not have an identity. I was just Hope, no true existence…just a person who was born only to die never to experience love or happiness in this life. I was dead on the inside, a mere existence of a person.

I wanted to die because there had to be something better on the other side than what I was going through almost daily. I spent many days daydreaming about how my life would be without fear, anxiety, and worry of the occurrence of the next beating. The truth of the matter is my daydreams of peace did not come true and there was always another beating from my mother.

Those words my mother spoke to me as I stood in the living room crushed me. At the time, I did not know what a prostitute was but I knew on the inside that it could not be good. Why? Because I remember how it felt when I heard her words and the look on my mother's face when she said them to me. I was young, but I felt like a ton of bricks fell on me. It was the first time I knew my mother hated me.

The look in her eyes was scary and uninviting. She truly did not want to have anything to do with me. How could that be? I was her first-born child, she was supposed to nurture, protect, and teach me. Little did I know God was designing me for greater things; I did not realize those words that were designed for me to fail could become so fruitful in my life. The words spoken was not only for my destruction, but it was also my destiny!

I grew up in James Island, SC, in a place affectionately known as "Down the Island". We lived on a dead-end dirt road bearing our family name in a small fixer-upper house. Even though it was the late seventies, we did not have any indoor plumbing and was one of the few houses that had an outhouse and a water pump in the front yard. I still remember the taste of the water from the pump; it was always a cool, sweet, and pure taste. Our home had a wooden stove and a fireplace that got very drafty in the wintertime.

I remember lizards frequently came into the house from the chimney. I recall one incident with my aunt so clearly. She was cleaning the chimney one day and a lizard crawled into her clothing. She came into the house screaming and ripping off her clothing. The lizard came running out of her pants and I ran screaming. Ever since that day, whenever I see a lizard…well you can imagine. That fear has never left me. If I saw a lizard in the house, I could not sleep until I knew it was dead or out the house. Today, I will go to a hotel; the lizard could have the house until I contact an exterminator.

Everyone around us seemed to flourish; they had nice cars and houses. Our house was the poorest on the block and we never owned a car. We did not have a lot, but it was home. Walking everywhere gave me character. I never went without a belly full and comfortable place to sleep. Still until this day, I recall some fond memories living on that dirty dusty road.

We lived on the family tract and life was good because there was always something to do and plenty of cousins to hang around. Softball, basketball, hide-n-go seek, hopscotch and other child hood games were played regularly.

My grandmother worked at the elementary school as a custodial worker. She did not make a lot of money, only minimum wage, but we always had something to eat and a roof over our heads. I was her first-born grandchild and I knew she loved me. When I was little, I often slept in her bed or on the floor in her bedroom. There was not a lot of space in that old house we lived in, however, grandmamma always made room for her family.

I always felt safe with her because she did her best to protect me from her daughter, my mother. For the most part, she was caught up between the love she had for her child and the love she had for her grandchild. She would often say "leave that girl alone, don't beat that child like that, and look at what you did to her". I would often hear my mother say, "I don't care, she deserved it".

I remember her telling me a story of when I was a baby and how she had come home to find my mother and aunt with "Babies for Sale" signs at the end of the street we were living on. They never tried that event again. My grandmother shut their shop down when she got off from work. She laughs now about the situation but she told me, it was not funny to her back then.

My grandmother was a hard-working, independent woman; she was the breadwinner and the head of the household. I admired her strength and tenacity.

She was everything to me. As her first-born grand-child, I felt a special connection to her. I used to pray that she did not have to go to work so she would be home to protect me. That dream never came true. I would wonder where God was and why He had not punished my mother for all she continually did to me.

I realize now how selfish that prayer was because she was the one we all looked to for guidance. She had to go to work because the bills rolled around every month like clockwork. I have very fond memories of her in the kitchen singing the song "*Jesus Be a Fence All Around Me*". She was a great singer. Her strong voice would make you want to shout the praises unto Almighty God. My grandmother was the first to teach me about God. She was the first that taught me how to pray. I love my grandmamma dearly. She sang that song so much until I adopted it as my life's theme song. I still sing it the way she did with my own words in my kitchen.

My grandmother went to church regularly but she could not take all of us with her. Although, I didn't go to church the song "Jesus Be A Fence" meant so much to me. I use to sing the song so much I got tired of singing it. I wanted the Jesus my grandmother knew to build fences around me. I wanted to be protected forever from my mother. I would often sing the song and imagine a fence around me. I would see my mother trying to get to me but she could not because the fence had a force field around it. Only those with special power could enter in and that power was simple, they had to love me.

I never heard things like "you're beautiful" or that "I was smart", even though I made good grades in school. I spent a lot of time alone listening to music, which became my outlet and my comfort. I had an old beat-up black radio. It did not have an antenna so I made one out of a wire-hanger. The reception was poor in my bedroom. I remember I had to lay it down on the windowsill to get a good reception. I would sing for hours alone in my room that I shared with my brothers.

I was a daydreamer, love to read books because I had the ability to use my imagination. I believed I was the character being rescued from this troubled life. The problem with daydreaming for me was that the reality of being abused often came to mind and brought me quickly back to my senses. Yet again, another beating occurred because I breathed a funny way when I passed her in the hallway…exactly what I am thinking, a stupid reason. For her, she had the ultimate control, power, and hold over me.

There was no reason for the abuse I suffered. I did not know most times what triggered my mother to put her hands on me. She was mean and surly when it came to her first-born child.

Flashback: We were living in a small rented house on Honey Hill. One night, very late, one of our cousins (although I did not know at the time) had come in through a broken window off the living room (apparently many people knew about that window).

My bedroom was off the living room and I shared it with my brothers. I laid frozen by a large figure in our bedroom standing at the foot of my bed. At first, I thought I was dreaming, but I was not because I pinched myself hard. I noticed him facing my two young brothers that were asleep in the other bed. I was concerned about my brothers because he was focused on them. He walked over to their bed, starring at them, and I forced myself to cough. He walked out the room quickly but came back and walked over to my brothers once again.

Every time he came into my bedroom and began walking to their bed, I coughed or mixed up in my bed. I moaned or talked as if I was having a dream. He would leave the room for a while but would return a few moments later.

After a cycle of coming and going, he did not return in our room. I acted on impulse and I got up and put my brothers in my bed. Frozen with fear not knowing who it was in the house, how he got in, or where he was, I could not scream out; I tried to scream, believe me. Too scared to run to my mother's room she shared with her boyfriend in the front of the house I stayed put because I needed to take care of my brothers.

The next morning I heard my mother coming to our room to awaken us for school. I was already up as I never went back to sleep. I could hear the man asleep on the couch as he snored loudly. Still afraid for my brothers I waited. I heard her call the man's name and asked him what he was doing in her house. I did not hear his response because they had walked in the kitchen to the front door. I checked my brothers and made sure they were all right.

As I walked to the bathroom, suddenly my mother cut me off and she accused me of letting our cousin in the house. That is what he told her. I told her I did not I was asleep and before I could say anything else, I was on the floor. She had punched me in the mouth. I did not know what happened for a few moments. She yelled out "I can't stand a lying ass child, you make me sick". My lip instantly swole and was bleeding. It is amazing with such a hard hit I did not lose any teeth. My mouth was definitely in pain for a few days.

My mother sent me to school that day with my lip split and swollen. I couldn't believe she allowed me to leave the house that way; but not without instructions. She instructed, if my teachers or friends asked what happened to me; I am to tell them I had fallen and hit my mouth on the floor. She would do the crime but did not want to pay the time. I followed her command exactly because I was terrified of her.

I loved my mother dearly regardless of how she treated me because she was my mother. I could not understand why she could not love me the same way. What was wrong with me? Was I not pretty enough? Why weren't I good enough? I saw the way she treated my brothers, why couldn't she pretend that I was boy? For a long time, I could not understand how a woman could have a baby and not fall in love with her baby instantly.

I resented my brothers in many ways because they had the pleasure of a mother who worshipped the ground they walked on. If they did something wrong I took their punishment because I was the oldest. I could not have friends over. I was not allowed to hang with my friends since everyone was "hot in their pants" and did not have any manners. My brothers rarely stayed indoors and visited their friends often.

I looked forward to the visitations at my grandmother's house because at least there I had my cousin and aunt to play with. Sometimes they would be cruel to me and teased me about my mother. I know it is because they did not understand abuse and at the time neither did I. I just knew what I was going through did not feel good; in fact, it felt very wrong.

At my grandmother's home, I had peace and an opportunity to laugh and be a kid. It was at my grandmother's that I felt safe and loved even though she worked us kids hard with the chores. She also allowed us to be kids at the same time. It was the only place I felt I had any balance in my life.

My grandmother would punish us when we did wrong but not severely and not always physically. She did a lot of threatening and she would spare our butts sometimes because she was too tired. Oh, I longed for those days living with my mother. She however only operated in one mode when it came to me. She was never tired for a beating.

The thing is I believe she loved me in her own twisted way just expressing her love was unbearable for me. I only associated her love with punishment since it was constant in our relationship. I prayed that I would grow up quickly and get away from my mother's wrath. I had to if I was going to survive. I believe I would be dead if I did not have a Savior who loved me unconditionally.

I am Hope; my godmother could not have picked a name more fitting for the kind of life I have lived. I have moved from a hopeless state to living IN Hope because I am a survivor. The devil knew the plans that God had for my life; he knew I would have much to overcome. He also knew my destiny would be great.

I love God and although not perfect, I strive to live in perfection every day. I still have some struggles with accepting love, but each day I understand it better by and by. God has truly given me beauty for my ashes and He has turned my mourning into dancing.

CHAPTER TWO

For the first few years of my life, I lived in the family home. My great-grandfather affectionately known to everyone as "Papa" lived in a small house behind us. He was up in age and never turned on any air conditioning. We kids would go there for the five ring butter cookies. Every now and then, he would get the lemon-flavored cookies, which was a special treat for me.

I remember we Papa's old rusty water pump in his front yard. We would pump the water and drink until our bellies poked out. The water from his pump would always be cool, it tasted like it came from the refrigerator. That's how cold it was. The cookie along with that water was often a highlight for me during the summer months. Granddaddy Papa also had fruit and nut bearing trees in his yard and during the appointed times of the year we would go and raid his plum and pecan trees.

It was important to my grandmother that we visited with her father so she insisted that we see him on a regular basis. I enjoyed visiting with granddaddy Papa and sometimes would go by myself to check on him and of course win brownie points.

Then one day he was not around, he became sick and could no longer stay in the house. At the time, it seemed like a big secret. Where did he go? I did not understand what was happening. The adults in my family did not seem to think that we needed to be a part of the grieving process. All I heard one day was that my granddaddy Papa had died.

It was my first encounter with death and even until this day, I remember the sadness I felt because I never got the opportunity to say goodbye. I was not allowed to attend the funeral so it was a very difficult time for me. It was a significant loss for me because he never harmed me. I grew a fear that the one person who I could count on to protect me would die. For weeks, I could not sleep due to nightmares that my grandmother would die and leave me here to be killed by my mother.

I remember praying softly that she (my mother) would die first so I would be safe. It was not long after the passing of my granddaddy Papa we moved and that is when my life flipped upside down. It was during this time that the family split. My mother moved into her own place around the corner from us.

At least for a while I was safe because she allowed me to stay with my grandmother. She visited often and the experience was not always good. When my grandmother was not around, she would threaten me for no reason.

Flashback: I remember one incident before we moved out of our old house. My sister's father was staying over and they were sleeping on the floor in the living room. I walked in to watch cartoons; my mother awoke and told me to get out, and I turned the TV off and went back in my grandmother's bedroom where I slept.

The next thing I knew I was punched and thrown around the room. She was yelling that I had disrespected her. She claimed I walked fast and sucked my teeth. I tried to get under the covers and even put pillows on me. At one point, I tried to take refuge under the bed, but she pulled me out with force. She slammed me on the bed, my head hit the post of the bed, and I saw my blood. It caused me to panic. I thought I was going to die.

I was screaming so loudly until finally my aunt woke up, ran in, and tried to protect me but my mother just tossed her like a pillow. I remember my aunt yelling my mother's name and begging her to stop. She told my mother, she is going to tell my grandmother and call the police on her. Because of my aunt, she stopped punching me. My mother then got into a physical altercation with my aunt. I sobbed so hard from the throbbing pain and the blood coming from my head.

My aunt's daughter came to me and she tried to console me. I was only six years of age but I recall it as if it were yesterday. It was the first time that my mother physically assaulted me. It would turn out to be one of the most memorable events of my life. I cannot believe I survived that beating or those that followed.

During that time, I did not know what abuse was and I really believe neither did the other adults in the house. My mother was a powerful woman; she had a lot of physical strength, built like a warrior. I used to think she was the man of the family as her reputation for brutality far exceeded the walls of the family. I mean as a kid, I thought she was kin to King Kong. I would imagine that large anomaly of an animal and my mother in cahoots trying to devour me.

I do not have the pleasure of saying I was a "happy go lucky" kid. I do not have the pleasure of saying I had the most wonderful parents in the world that nurtured me, read me bed time stories, took me to the park, played ball with me, or let me be a princess. There were no family trips or visitations to my school.

I can continue with things I missed in my childhood. The point of the matter, I did not have the life many of my friends experienced.

All I knew as a child was hurt and more hurt; I only existed in a shell of a person. People saw me every day, but they did not know that all they were seeing was an empty looking glass. If they had turned me over, nothing would pour out. Love is a commodity that no child should lack. No child should ever experience love in a negative way.

The dysfunction that stems from the lack of love is penetrating to the soul. Trust, sincerity, faith in God, and others are hard to except, at least it was in my case. I heard my mother say I love you to my brothers but not express her love to me. I associated her love with physical abuse and neglect.

I recall telling myself she loved me because she physically and verbally abused me. I could not understand why a mother who carried her baby to term, they were inseparable for nine months, could not love and nurture her child. It has to be that love was not all that. In my world, that was what I believed. I had three younger siblings; my sister was given away at a few months of age to other relatives. My sister was the lucky one, she was secure with people who loved her and treated her well. She grew up with stability and security I only dreamt I could have.

My brothers were treated as kings as they never lacked for nothing. They had all the Tonka, Kenmore, Lego blocks and Hess trucks they could stand. My mother hated dolls, and whenever I received a doll she would take it, rip its head off, and bury it. She would threaten me that if she saw me with a doll she would beat my behind.

I resented and loved my brothers very much. I never wanted them to experience the pain and suffering I endured at the hands of our mother. They never did because my mother worshipped the ground they walked on. Apparently, she was capable of loving and extending love but i was not blessed to receive her love.

I lived in a very quiet world trying not to disturb my mother in anyway and blend in with my brothers as much as I could. They were her life and I knew it well as they received simple pleasures I was not privy too. I prayed even though I did not know God personally, "please let me grow up and earn a lot of money and I would just buy all the love I would ever need in this life". It was a child's prayer since I am now thirty-nine and still seek the love and affection of my mother. As I grew older, people would encourage me and tell me to let my mother go. They advised me to live for myself and take care of my children. For whatever reason, I have not given up hope that I would experience my mother's love, it could still happen.

CHAPTER THREE

Flashback: As I stated earlier we lived in an old drafty house. By today's building codes, it would be condemned, but it was home. I remember the old wood stove in the kitchen area. The family would gather around it to warm themselves. I loved that old wood stove because it kept the entire front rooms of the house toasty.

One morning my grandmother was in the kitchen cooking breakfast, she was singing one of her spiritual songs. She was praising and worshipping the Lord on that very cold morning. My grandmother was humming and moaning from the depths of her belly. She was a great songtress and her singing could soothe anyone's soul, especially mine. I loved to hear my grandmother hum and sing. She should have been on stage with Mahalia Jackson, one of the greatest singers that ever lived.

My mother had came home from Job Corps for a few days. As I walked to the kitchen I noticed my aunt was still in bed asleep. My first cousin was asleep next to her. I did as I normally did on a cold winter morning and joined my grandmother in the kitchen and stood by the wood stove. The fire was roaring; she had put fresh pieces of wood in the stove. The kitchen was nice and toasty. My grandmother was humming and cooking breakfast. She was stirring the grits as my mother entered in the kitchen. It looked like she was not in a good mood, but to me that was nothing new. Every time my mother came near me, my anxiety-level went off the meter.

I was in the kitchen listening to the sweet sound of my grandmother's voice, warming by the stove, and salivating for her breakfast. My mother stood directly in front of me at the stove, staring me down. Her gaze was penetrating. I did my best not to make eye contact with her; I could see the evil in her eyes. She said something to me but I do not recall her exact words. Before I could move, my mother grabbed my left arm and laid it on the hot stove. I screamed with sheer pain and horror. I saw my grandmother grab her and slammed her to the floor. My aunt came running out of her room and scooped me up in her arms. She yelled, "Why the hell you did this to this child? I'm going to call the police and lock your ass up."

I was screaming as my aunt poured cool water on my wrist. She tried to stop me from yelling but the burn hurt so badly. I heard my mother yell out "That's my f**ing child and all of y'all better remember that, sheen goin' disrespect me". My grandmother slapped her hard and told her to get out of her house. In the meantime, my auntie began rubbing butter on my arm, doing all she can to comfort me and soothe the burn.

My grandmother came to me and said, "Girl your momma is crazy". My auntie held my head close to her chest as my grandmother assessed the burn. They did not call the police because that is not something black folks do. Everything that happens in the family stays within the family. My grandmother told me she was going to get "papers" on me, meaning she would file for custody. Unfortunately, that never occurred and the abuse continued until the day I planned to end my life.

Flashback: Christmas was once a holiday I dreaded growing up. One vivid year, I cried so hard because I had not received a gift. My grandmother worked hard, but could not afford to buy me anything. I watched heartbroken as my first cousin and aunt (she's younger than I am) opened up their gifts. My grandmother trying to comfort me said, "Biscuit (that's what they call my mother) didn't get Hopie anything, and that's a crying shame".

My aunt said, "I told Biscuit to buy that girl something because Hopie daddy gave her money but Biscuit said no, she was not getting her anything for Christmas because she didn't have no money." Funny, since my little brother got some Hess and yellow Tonka trucks.

An older cousin who had stopped by to wish everyone a Merry Christmas inquired what was wrong with me. My aunt responded by telling her that I did not receive anything for Christmas. She hugged me and left. I was upset but began to calm down since my cousin and aunt allowed me to play with their toys.

My cousin returned to the house with a small package of seven-inch white dolls and gave them to me. I was ecstatic. I can still see those dolls long blonde hair dressed in blue and white outfits. I was so happy to have a gift that was mine; it dried up my tears until my mother took the dolls and destroyed them. The Christmas season growing up was always a hard time for me. I made a promise that when I had children they would never know that pain.

My mother destroyed my dolls by pulling their heads off and throwing them in the trash. I have not forgotten the joy of receiving them nor the lessons of sharing and giving. I have learned the value of the following statement; "it's the thought that counts".

My mother always rationalized about not buying me new clothes, getting my hair done, or providing my basic needs. For this reason, I truly thank God for a grandmother and an aunt who were there for me. They did their best to do what was necessary in order for me to live.

I was un-churched; I did not know my mother's relationship with God. All I knew was we did not attend church when I was a child. I did not know (what I do now) about the basic tenets of faith, hope, and love. We did not have family dinners or outings that fostered love or solidified the family. My parents were not married to each other and their relationship status has not changed. My parents did not like each other and the two of them in a marriage would have been atrocious.

I had two voids in my life, the alienation of affection and not knowing Jesus Christ. The feelings of neglect and rejection are real; the effects from those emotions can be life-long. Even now at times, I struggle emotionally with my love walk, trusting people with my heart content, and approval addiction. I want everyone to like me because I do my best to "esteem others" above myself. What I have come to know is that is not always the case; people will not love me just because I extend love to them.

I am a master at wearing masks, hiding my true

feelings and covering up pain, all which stemmed from my upbringing. I did not want my mother to get into any trouble with the law because I was fearful for my life. She told me often "she brought me into this world and would take me out." I hid the bruises from my teachers, friends, and even family members.

There were several occasions as I grew older, that my loving grandmother reported the abuse but nothing seemed to prevail. Similarly, I called the police to report the abuse but nothing worked. My mother was great at talking herself out of trouble. Often times, she put the blame on me; the police officers that investigated would let her slide. I could not understand how officers who were suppose to protect me allowed my mother to get away with abuse.

It was because of police officers she was invincible and I worked to do whatever it took not to offend my mother in anyway. Here is the thing with abusers: anything can be construed as disrespect or getting out of line. I declare even to this day my mother made things up just so she could beat me. I think it was a way of working off her frustrations because she was so unhappy with her life.

Flashback: For example, my mother did not allow me to go anywhere. She knew we had two young women (neighbors) who were in high school that I admired. They were very pretty and had the life I only dreamed about having. Living above their father's store, I watched them from a distant wishing they would notice me. I can testify that when they did notice me they welcomed me in their life. The sisters were good neighbors for me to know and learn from. I do not know if they knew what was going on at our house, but they were always nice to me. I pray that God gives me the chance one day to tell them how truly wonderful I believe them to be. One day my mother allowed me to go next door and spend some time with them; their house was cool and beautifully decorated.

I believe they allowed me to be in their presence because I had grown on them. After spending the day with my neighbors, I returned home. My mother was standing at the end of the steps with a leather belt and hit me across the face with it. She accused me of being down the street with a girl she did not like only because she believed the girl was promiscuous.

My mother stated someone came to the house and told her I had gone down the street and not next door. She did not walk next door to check if it was true, she believed the "someone." I screamed for dear life, because the belt hit me in the eye. My eye instantly swelled shut and blood came out my nose. My face was burning from the thick leather belt.

I could hardly see to get upstairs so I could go and hide under my bed. The hits kept coming; they were fierce. I finally made it to my room and I dove under my bed. It was at that time she got the broom and began jabbing me in my side and back with such force, I felt like dying. Every thrust felt like that broom handle was going to break my skin and take out one of my organs.

Finally, she stopped, and I stayed under my bed. I had to be sure she would not return to finish the job. I stayed under the bed so long, that I fell asleep; too afraid to leave my safe place. I was there for hours and it was nighttime before I ventured on the top of my bed. My whelps were stinging me and oozing blood, my left eye was throbbing so bad all I could do is cry. It was swollen shut. I only had sight out of one eye.

Except for going to the bathroom, I stayed out of my mother's way. I did not make a sound, she did not offer me dinner and I did not ask to eat. The next morning when I awoke, she saw me and told me that I could not go to school. She also stated she found out that I was next door all day and had not been down the street. She whipped me for nothing; the near loss of my eye and the pain from the broom, endured over nonsense.

My mother never apologized for beating me the way she did that day but she made sure to warn me not to tell anyone or it would get worse. If I had not taken cover, God only knows what might have happened that Saturday. I might not be living today, but God was on my side, I just did not know it.

CHAPTER FOUR

Flashback: I was about nine years old and we caught a ride "down the island" to visit with my grandmother. Oh how I loved seeing my grandmamma, cousins, and aunt who is younger than I am. When we arrived, my grandmother asked me how I was doing and how was my mother treating me.

I was cautious when my mother was around with what I shared with my grandmother. My mother did not care who was around when she got angry with me; I felt her anger in a bad way. I said, "Grandmamma I didn't sleep well because I heard strange noises that frightened me." I told her the noises were coming from near my mother's room, and my heart was beating fast. I just laid still because I thought something was in the house.

My grandmother asked me how did the noise sound. It was high pitched and squeaky. She told me it might have been rats. I did not know what sexual noises sounded like. All I know is that my mother had overheard what my grandmother was saying to me. She confronted me, "what noises your ass is talking about?"

I told her I did not know and next thing I knew, I was on the floor. She had punched me in the mouth and accused me of not minding my own business. She stomped on me and I screamed out, "oh Lord help me she is going to kill me, I said I'm sorry I didn't know what was happening." My grandmother and aunt tried to stop her from stomping me to death. What her hand did not touch, her feet did; my head hitting that wood floor gave me an instant headache. I curled up like an infant trying to protect my face, head, and stomach from the kicks.

Oh, how I cried and finally my grandmother pulled her off me and she told me to run and that is what I did. I ran and hid in the woods. I knew my grandmother would call when it was safe. At the time, I honestly didn't know what I had said, that got her so angry. It was not until a few years later after I learned about the birds and bees; that I had overheard a private moment between her and her boyfriend.

My cousin ran out the house with me, and a short

time later, I heard my grandmother calling me to return. I had scratches on my legs from the wood floor, my mouth was swollen and few nicks on my face. As we were returning, my cousin said, "girl your momma tried to kill you." When we arrived at the house, I was too scared to enter in and my cousin went in first to see where my mother was. She came back and told me our mothers left and went to the club around the corner.

My grandmother coerced me to come in by telling me she would not let my mother touch me again. I went in and she had the alcohol ready to clean me up, or as she said, "kill the germs and take down the swelling". It was an excruciating pain as she poured alcohol on my wounds. I cried because it burned so badly. She was very gentle and careful as she cared for me.

After she cleaned me up, she laid me on the couch and allowed me to watch anything I wanted on television. She also assured me that she was going to take me away from my mother and "finish raising me." I am sad to say that day never came, not until I became suicidal, but that is another chapter.

It amazes me as I am writing this book. Its surreal how many scenarios still play out in my mind. It is as if my mind is a movie reel, and it plays my life story repeatedly. The same thing with the words spoken; the tape recorder rewinds and playback every segment. I believe that is because God wants the story to be told as a testament of His goodness, grace, and tender mercy. He is not a respecter of persons and deserves all the glory for the great things He has done, is doing, and will do in my life.

I share my testimony no matter how much the enemy says, "Don't write that because people will judge you." Being vulnerable and telling my very secret past is a testament to the goodness of Jesus. After all, He died on a shameful, old rugged cross for me; He did it just for me at Calvary. My commercial break is over for now.

Flashback: I will never forget one Friday morning as I went off to school, I told my mother I would be going to grandma's house after school for the weekend. That was normal for me until that particular day. I went to James Island Middle School at the time, and when I arrived to grandma's house, she was at work. My cousin and I were in the house when some of her friends and our relatives stopped by to see my cousin. They were standing on the outside laughing and talking when my mother showed up. I was in the house watching them from the living room window. They were standing on the outside talking to my cousin when my mother showed up.

My cousin noticed immediately that my mother

was not in a good mood. As I looked, I saw her slam the door of the car she had ridden in through the sheer curtains. My heart raced so fast I felt sick and I began to panic. I was frozen in my steps as I had seen that death look before. I cried out, "Lord, please don't let her kill me," and I ran out the back door. I ran in the woods while my cousin tried to stop her. I could hear her yelling, "I'm going to kill you if you run from me."

Not aware what I had done. All I could do is run as fast I could and as far in the woods as I could. In fact, I could hear them yelling; "keep running Hopie, keep running girl and hide, we are coming." I ran until I was out of breath and out of gas, I tried to hide under a thick brush and for a while, she could not find me. However, when she did, the Lord showed me mercy (she didn't kill me).

My mother found me and dragged me by my feet on my back from out the bush as the sticky burrows ripped open my back. I screamed for sheer pain! Somehow, I became entangled in the blackberry patch and a part of the vine wrapped around my neck scratching me deeply. (Even now, when I arch my neck I can see traces of the scratches from the sticky bush). The more she pulled, the deeper the vine penetrated my skin. That was not enough for her; she stopped pulling me and began punching and kicking me re-peatedly. All I could do was put myself in the fetal position and pray "God don't let her kill me please I'm not ready to die, help me".

My mother became angered by my screams for my cousins to help. She told me if I did not stop she would take my life right then and there, but I couldn't stop because she was pounding me. Finally, my cousin and her friends found us and pulled her off me but not before, she stomped me one last time. As they dragged her away, I laid there exhausted and sobbing.

I was dirty, humiliated, bleeding and petrified that she would one day kill me. In addition, I was a bit relieved by the thought that one day God may let me die so that I would not feel this pain anymore. They carried me to the house and tried to take care of me as best as possible. We didn't have a phone so my cousin went across the street to call grandmamma to come home from work.

Before that day, my cousin never cried for me, but that day she sobbed bitterly for me. Even her friends expressed their sorrow for not being able to do more. They were in shock because they had no idea my mother was that violent. I had become a master by this time; I knew how to hide the wounds, lie about the bruises, and remain quiet about what really went on at home. I learned the art of masking at an early age.

My grandmother could not leave work because

she did not have a ride home. When she arrived home and saw me, she immediately called the police. When the police arrived, they stated there was nothing they could do because my mother was not around. My grandma was livid. She could not believe there were no laws on the books that could keep me safe. It seemed she would have to kill me before she would ever be arrested for abusing me.

I am now a thirty-nine year old woman who still seeks the purist form of love from others. I am not saying that I know how to love perfectly; I have simply learned the true essence of love. True love does not warrant performance, it accepts us the way we are. God loves me for who I am. He accepted me while I was still in my mother's womb. Accepting Jesus into my life has healed many wounds in my mind, heart, and spirit. I have learned on this journey of life, the enemy cannot control nor harm me the way he once did.

CHAPTER FIVE

Guilt and shame is what I lived with for most of my early childhood and teenage years. Guilt is a funny emotion that binds a person's state of being. I felt guilty because I must have done something that caused my mother to react the way she did. Why couldn't I stop being the person that set her off? Did I speak too much? Was I not cute enough?

I spent many days and nights wondering what was wrong with me. It did not matter how well behaved I was in school or at home. It did not matter how good my grades were or how many accolades I received. I simply did not feel loved by the one human being who should have loved me with no conditions.

No child should ever have to question whether their parents love them or have their best interests at heart. It was very lonely growing up in a house where there were no conversations with me, no real time to play outdoors and just be a kid. My mother stole my childhood from me. I believe she did not have a loving childhood and did not know how to provide a normal upbringing for me. She was not a nurturer because she was not nurtured. As I got older I saw the interaction between my mother, grandmother and my mother's siblings; I began to gain a better understanding why she "ticked" the way she did.

I considered my mother mean and heartless and for many years, I hated her. I even prayed for her to die. I was tired of the beatings, the put downs had taken its toll on me. I started to believe I was worthless and did not deserve to live anymore. This was the start of me becoming suicidal and putting a plan into motion to end this nothing of a life.

I remember one time she told me I was adopted and I was so excited. I questioned her about my real mother. Truly, my real mother was not aware of what was going on in her little girl's life. She would not have given me to someone who secretly desired to kill me simply because I was born a female. As I stated earlier in the book, she made it very clear to me she hated girl children. What a penalty I had to pay because God had given me life inside of her.

I used to question God a lot about His love for me

and if He loved me why did He give me these parents? I remember crying out to Him a lot as a young person and I did not knew who He was. My mother did not go to church and was not concerned that her children go and learn about their Savior.

You see my mother had a number of companions all whom I witnessed beat her severely. As young as I was, and regardless of what I had suffered from her hands, I did my best to defend her from her abusers. I have had a rifle put in my face and a finger almost bitten off trying to protect her. I did not want her to be hurt. Although, I tried to help her she often turned on me, after he apologized to her and all was good again between them. Many nights, I was awakened out of my sleep to the cursing and fighting. It was chaos. Sometimes it sounded like the walls were being punched but my mother was the punching bag.

My baby brother was a toddler and he would scream so loud, "STOP IT" "stop hitting my mama!" His cry immediately sent me into protective mode. I did not care if I got hurt; I wasn't going to allow anyone to bring harm to my baby brother. My mother would say that she was fine and demand us to go back to bed. But really who did she think could sleep when the pounding sounds of her being hit sounded like a freight train? Nevertheless, this lifestyle became a part of my life, as it was a regular occurrence especially after they had a night out on the town.

Oftentimes, I was left at home to babysit my brothers. I was given a long list of rules of what we could not touch which mounted to everything. Although my mother received public assistance and child support from our dad, we could not touch anything because it belonged to her man. I made a mental note never to treat my children (if I ever have children) that way.

Life was crazy. I did not have another place to live and the adults often made promises they did not keep. I just knew if I made it to adulthood, my life would be different. The day was coming when this life would be over…or so I thought.

CHAPTER SIX

I grew up with several men who wanted to be my father, but those men hurt my mother. I did not meet my biological father until I was seven years old. Before then, I called another man "daddy" because he was good to my little brother and me. Even after he and my mother broke up, he always accepted us as his children. It was devastating to learn that he was not my biological father.

I am writing about my biological father in this chapter. When I share, my testimony people always ask me where my father was while I was being abused from my mother. From the time I knew myself, all I heard about my father was that he was no good. He was a deadbeat that did nothing for my brother and me. I was an adult when I discovered it was a lie concerning my dad. My parents did not like each other and they downgraded one another.

My father shared with me a few years ago, that if he had known what my mother did to me he would have taken custody of me. I believe him. Although he neglected me emotionally, I loved my father more than I loved my mother. I did not have him to turn to and protect me. Unless it was Christmas, a few sightings at the softball field, or the social club, I did not see him. He was not the knight and shining armor father of my dreams.

During our conversation, I could not bring myself to tell him about the sexual molestation. Even at thirty-six years of age, telling my father that another man touched and hurt his only daughter was too much for me. He will learn about the horrible event by reading my story. I no longer live in shame about what happened. I now know I was a young girl who "filled out:" as a woman earlier than most girls my age and what happened to me is not my fault. Telling my father would have made me feel more ashamed because of the guilt and shame that came along with sexual abuse. I did not have that close father-daughter relationship with my father. I could not tell him the truth of what was happening in my life because I felt discredited as his daughter.

My parents did not attend church. Honestly, I do

not know if they are believers. I do not know if they have ever confessed Christ as their personal Savior and I will not speculate. God is the only judge and last time I checked, He did not need my help. There is nothing concerning faith I learned from my parents.

I do not recall either of them praying, praising, or even instructing us as children to have faith in Christ. However, they are the parents God gave me, and I respect them regardless. "Honor thy mother and thy father," the Good Book says, so that is what I aspire to do.

I have few memories of my father in my childhood. Even after he revealed to my brother and I, he was our real father, he did not convey his love for us. I could not believe it. I whispered to God, "Really Lord, I have two parents who doesn't care about me?" The one man I knew loved me I was being forced to no longer acknowledge.

I never forgot daddy or the nickname "Chumpy" he affectionately called me. Nevertheless I had to comply and accept he was not my true father because I was only a child. However, when I got the opportunity to see the man I knew as daddy I rejoiced, he's always been kind and good to me.

I was about nine years old, I was washing my grandmother's glass ashtrays and one of them broke in the sink. He was there for me. He rushed me to the hospital and talked me through the doctors removing the glass and stitching me up. On the way home he assured me I would be fine and he's there if I ever needed him. He was a good dad. Even now, he acknowledges me as his daughter. After the incident with my hand, I did not see much of the man I knew as daddy. Sadly, as time went on he stopped coming around and we lost touch.

My biological father is a hardworking man; he is a quiet man unless he is drinking. For as long as I have known him, he has been gainfully employed and independent. I believe my brother and I follow our father's example of working hard and taking care of our business. He is definitely not the bum my mother had me believing. I grew up thinking that he had not financially supported my brother and me. I thought he had my mother struggling with his only children. My father kept the receipts from his child support payments. He showed them to me about five years ago; now I truly know he always cared for his children.

I am grateful for the talk we had a few years ago. It was a relief as he listened to the cry of my heart. I know he truly loves his only daughter. He would have probably hurt my mother if he knew she abused me. We have been building our relationship, and it is a wonderful journey. We do not talk everyday or even

every week, but when we do talk, it is always pleasant. He says I want to be the boss because I care about
his health. I do not want anyone doing for him what I
can do because he is my daddy. I love him.

CHAPTER SEVEN

We moved quite a few times and lived in several areas of James Island. We were always moving for one reason or another it seem. I was transferred from school to school. Making and maintaining friends was difficult. As the new kid on the block, I often was teased for my looks and how I dressed. The boys were especially brutal to me. Girls who I thought were my friends would set me up to be picked on. They too would team up together and bully me. I was an easy target because I had no voice and lived in fear of people.

I must admit as ruthless as my mother was to me she could not stand kids picking on me. I recall one incident when she slapped one of the boys for picking on me at the bus stop. I was quiet and reserve as some children become whom suffer from abuse; too afraid to act out or defend themselves for fear of being hurt.

The physical abuse left me alone and afraid. I could not confide in anyone about my abuse. I was terrified and it was drilled in me not to tell our deepest family secret. What occurred in our house was no one's business. It was difficult to understand why no one became the voice for Hope, the person who would advocate for me and stop the abuse. Family and school officials would ask me "what happened to your face? Alternatively, "where did you get that bruise from?" I lied and they did not involve themselves further with the matter.

Out of fear, I would lie and make up stories as to how I was injured, but no one inquired more or had a deeper intuition that I needed help. What perplexed me more were the family members whom witnessed the abuse. All they would say was, "you shouldn't have hit that girl like that or you really need to stop". They would say to her, "when that girl grow up she is going to buss your behind back. It makes no sense how you hit that girl over nothing."

There were times I witnessed my grandmother get in her face. In fact, they were involved in a few physical altercations because of how my mother treated me. My grandmother often said to me, "Hopie one day your momma is going to need you and when she does treat her with kindness." I would say within myself "she better hope she doesn't need me; I wouldn't even get her a glass of cold drinking water."

I was a toxic kid who was depressed and oppressed. One day all of those mixed up emotions turned suicidal. I was so sick and tired of being ridiculed. I am a person, not a punching bag or a doormat. I am her first-born, her daughter, is it too much to ask to be treated as one? All I wanted is her love. Instead, I was a child forced to grow up fast so I could protect myself and get away from her as quickly as possible.

I would spend hours alone plotting how to get away so she could never hurt me again. I would listen to my old raggedy radio, dream of an escape and the possibility of how good my life would be once I leave my mother's regime. I would get lost for hours in my thoughts. My thoughts were all I had as a child. It was the one place in my life that my mother could not fully dominate. Thoughts of her would enter my mind but I would banish them for trespassing.

I did not watch television unless my mother was not home. Using images from the television was not much of a reality to me. God gave me a vivid imagination. I escaped in my own world often, which helped me dull the pain of my childhood. I did not know Jesus or the power of prayer so I believe the Lord gave me imagination. He was taking care of me and I did not know it until years later.

Although the physical abuse was brutal on my body, I experienced something worse. This act was more evil than any beating I sustained at the hands of my mother. I could hide the bruises and tell lies about them but this act reached down in my soul. The action of this one person changed my worldview of life forever. I admit, I prayed hard, making the decision to write this book. I concluded the identity of my abuser is not as important as sharing my story of what happened to me and how I overcame. God delivered me and that is what I want the world to know. I am free and all praises I give to the Almighty, Everlasting Father in heaven.

Today, I have total peace and I have truly forgiven my abuser. The power of forgiveness did not allow me to forget but it did compel me to press on. The peace that I have gave me purpose, direction, and conviction to help others. I have come to an understanding of God's word in *Philippian 4:7* which says, *"And the peace of God, which surpasses all understanding, will guard your hearts and minds through Jesus Christ."*

It was years before I understood that I had been violated. At the time, I did not have a name for what hurt my body and heart so bad. However, I did knew that on the inside I felt physically ill from its effects.

Physical abuse was hard to endure but having my innocence stolen in the middle of the night was unbearable. Home was supposed to be safe and it became my haunting nightmare. I was taken advantaged of because he was older and stronger than I was.

I do not understand what causes a person to want to hurt another. I do not comphehend what possesses one relative to desire having sexual relations with another family member. Particularly, when that relative is vulnerable, fragile, smaller and younger. It is as a predator is to its prey, at the most opportune time, they pounce and destroy their prey. For me, even down to the time of night was chosen. I was always in a deep sleep but awoken into a nighmare. It didn't destroy my life completely. He had no clue he was messing with greatness.

Living with relatives can be a great experience particularly when you feel safe that is until your security is broken. In my case, I stopped feeling safe once my thief in the night started invading my body. Once that happened my thoughts became that it was better to be beaten than it was being touched. There was nothing pleasurable about being poked from behind. As I stated before, I have to share this part of my story because it happened; I am who I am because of it.

I lived in several places amongst different relatives. Moving around so much just became a part of my lifestyle. I would have been considered a nomad having slept in so many places. I never truly felt like I was at home in one stable place.

One particular relative's house that I stayed will never be forgotten because of the excruciating pain that rippled my body in the dark midnight hours. I am purposely not telling the specifics of the place because I have forgiven and am healed. Sexual abuse is ruthless and when it comes at the hands of a family member that makes it even more callous. It is a part of my testimony but the abuse no longer has a stronghold in my life. I thought I was in a safe place but I was too young to notice the eyes that were watching me.

You see, I developed early with a body as a grown woman. I believe my molester preferenced a certain part of my anatomy since that was the only part of me he violated. I would pray desperately "Lord please let him (my abuser) get in (make entrance inside of me) tonight so he would leave me alone". I wanted to scream and wake up the house but I could not scream paralyzed with fear that the blame would be placed upon me.

For several months, he took advantage of me. I hated for nightfall to come because I did not know when he would make his next attempt. I was always on edge and nervous at night. I hoped he would leave me alone. He did not violate me every night but often enough, I feared falling asleep. Staying awake did not help; he always waited until I fell in a deep sleep. He only wanted to penetrate me anally. It was very painful and degrading. I did not see his face but I could smell him. He came in, did his business as if I was trash and left as quietly as he entered my room. I still do not understand why I could not scream out or why I never told anyone.

I should have screamed but I was in shock, perplexed by the whole situation. I was terrified because I thought I had done something to turn him on. I took the coward way out and I bit down on the bed as hard as I could, biting my lips until they bled. I held the edge of the bed so hard my fingers turned numb until he was done. I would have no feelings in my hands for a while after the event and I did not want to feel. I just wanted him to do his business and get off me. I was a whore to him although I was a virgin.

I would cry, but he would tell me to stay quiet, so we did not wake anyone up. We? I thought to myself. He acted as if what he was doing to me was actually consensual. I was awoken from my peaceful sleep for this sick, twisted, ungodly act and he has the nerve to say "WE". I was not an active participant. I just did not have the courage or the voice to yell stop!

I did all I could to stop it. I would pretend that

I was dead so he would leave and not try to insert his instrument, but to no avail. I was as heavy as I could make myself so he could not move me, but that did not work. He was most strong when my body was lifeless and heavy. He managed to turn me over every time, pull my underwear off, and penetrate my innocence.

"How could this be happening?" I wondered, and "why did I let it keep happening?" Fear is a horrible, crippling emotion that will cause a person not to perform as they would normally. My relative (abuser) never threatened my life or stated he would harm me in any way if I told but I still feared him. I knew if I had told, the backlash from my family would have been too much for me to handle. It is crazy how paralyzed I was at the time, but I made myself a promise that I would never let another man violate me again. Fear crippled me back then and haunted my life for years…that is until the Lord stepped in and rescued me.

What I could not understand was how no one saw the personality changes within me. I became very angry, depressed, and withdrawn. I was in a dark hole. I felt empty and worthless. It was if I had died, yet I was still breathing. In my mind, I called myself all kinds of dirty names because that is how I felt, dirty. The lowest of the lowest; I was scum for letting it happen and a coward for not talking. I hated myself for not being strong enough to tell. I acted as if the abuse never occurred. I just pretended it was a bad dream. On the contrary, my most intimate sensitive place knew without a doubt, what had occurred repeatedly.

I was wounded significantly and had nowhere to turn for help. I went to school every day. There were no flyers or announcements. Not one teacher that talked about child molestation. No information of where a child in trouble could turn to for help. I lived in a very dark world, all alone; there was simply no one to confide in and no place to go. I was forced in an unknown world all because a family member violated me. He took a part of me every time he touched me. Still to this day, I cannot sleep in a dark room, nor tolerate being touched in certain ways because it triggers unpleasant memories.

In spite of everything, I made it through. I reached out to God for help. I was angry and I questioned him about my parents and abuser relative. Why were they that kind of people? My earthly father was alive yet I could not turn to him because of his constant drinking. I rarely ever saw him sober and we did not have that kind of a relationship. We did not converse. Fathers are supposed to make their daughters feel love, protected, and power to come to them when someone tries to hurt them. Simply, I did not have that type of father.

It is because of who my father is that I did not have the strength necessary to tell him. My fear was hearing him tell me it was my fault or deal with the fact that he would not believe me. It was easier to remain quiet and pray it would all end soon. I needed compassion and understanding and my father was not in a place where he could give me either of those things.

About a year later, I realized that physical abuse was better than the sexual abuse I endured. It was definitely more than I could bear as I was entering into my teenage years. I pondered in my heart that I would never talk about it. I would take the horrible secret to my grave...or so I thought.

God had another plan for my life. He has given me this testimony to help others who have suffered abuse. We can be free from the shame of what happened in the dark within our family. Today, our luggage of burdens can be unpacked as we confront and conquer the demons of our past. Our bio's can read, we have been healed in Jesus name. We are no longer victims because we are no longer ashamed and our past cannot hinder our present.

CHAPTER EIGHT

Once again, I moved and was returned to my mother and her current boyfriend. At least, for now, I would no longer be violated by my abuser relative. I would rather be beaten. My mother had not changed, nor had her situation with me. My nightmare continued until I was in high school and became suicidal. I had decided if there was a God, it was time for me to meet him. I needed to talk with him face to face about some things, mainly my life.

I heard great things about heaven such as it was beautiful, it is peaceful, pain does not exist there, and no more crying. I yearned most for a place like heaven and it was time for me to have peace, joy, and happiness. It was time for my body to finally, be at rest. We were living in a barn at the time. I never claimed this place as a home; it was home to my mother. It was the most embarrassing place I had ever lived. My father paid more than four hundred dollars a month but we could not live in a place with the necessities like a kitchen, sink, toilet, and a tub.

I was miserable because of the put downs and not being able to eat because everything was her man's. I was not allowed to go anywhere and did not socialize with the kids that lived around me. Picture a barn with no windows. I was in prison, isolated, and still sharing a room with my brothers. I had no privacy, a pee bucket was in our bedroom, and it was horrible. Yet my mother and her boyfriend seemed content especially since they were hardly at home. Their addiction to drugs kept them away most evenings. They were always out drinking, doping and fighting. He would beat her; she would find reasons to beat me. A vicious cycle and I needed to escape; I WANTED OUT.

I thought about running away without ceasing. Sadly, my mother made it clear, if I ran away, when the authorities brought me back, she would kill me. She knew how terrified I was of her and I took her threats seriously.

One day in school, the morning announcer announced that one of my classmates had died. She stated he had committed suicide and that counselors would be available all day to speak to students.

I pondered in my own heart how sad it was hearing about my classmate. I also thought how free he must feel, no more hurt and no more pain to contend with in this life. We had a moment of silence and I prayed that the Lord was taking care of him at that very moment. It was a very sad day at school as we mourned the loss of a friend and classmate.

Several months went by and I was still in contemplation of my own suicide because anything had to be better than how I was living. Suicide consumed my thoughts and I needed a good plan. I just wanted the pain in my heart to stop forever. My mother would remember she bore a daughter and her name was Hope. She would have to live the rest of her life in regret.

I wanted her to cry and mourn for me, but then again I did not believe she would care if I were no longer living. A woman who said her daughter would grow up to be nothing but a prostitute and amount to nothing did not have a heart. She hated having girl children. I wanted my death at my own hands to crush her and just maybe she would come to know the pain in my heart she bestowed upon me.

The bunk beds my brothers slept on were made of pure steel. It was the best thing to hang myself on. I started making my noose out of a wire hanger and hid it so no one would know what I was planning. I was sick and tired of my loveless life except for my brothers; they looked up to me and I kept them protected.

I hated I would have to leave them so soon; especially, my baby brother, who still needed his big sister because of his stuttering problem. I would help him pronounce his words. He slept in my bed every night; we are eleven and half years apart and it pained me deeply to have to leave him. In many ways, he looked up to me as his mother because I took care of my baby brother. I made sure he ate, bathed, played and made him feel safe. I was very protective of my two younger brothers; I would have hurt anyone who tried to harm them in any way.

I decided I was going to make one last attempt and appeal to my mother's heart by writing her a long letter. In that letter, I told her how I felt and how much I loved her but that I could not understand why she did not love me as she loved my brothers. I wished I had not wrote her that letter because when she read it she did not take what I said well at all. She slapped me knocking me to the floor and that sealed in my heart that death was my only way out of this turmoil life.

I sat down that night and wrote another letter to my first cousin and best friend. My best friend and I shared a locker at school, and the next morning when I arrived at school, I gave her the letter. I made her promise to keep it in the locker and not to read it until the next day. She kept pounding me but I made her swear not to touch the letter again until tomorrow. She assured me she would, and we went to our classes. At the end of the school day, the letter was still in our locker unopened.

I guess she knew I was up to something because she did not keep her promise. I knew she did not keep her promise when my aunt showed up at my house to take me away. I had everything ready and just as I was about to hang myself "But God" stopped by (I learned this after my conversion). She said that my best friend who was very upset brought the letter to her mom. She was afraid that I had already committed suicide; however, God intervened using her to break the trust between us.

I left with my aunt after she talked with my mother. The next day I went to school as usual. I was called to come to the front office and my mother was there. The guidance counselor and a social worker were talking. My mother took that liberty and said if I did not tell those damn people I was lying about her abusing me, something would happen to me. My heart was pounding so hard I could not think. Luckily, for me, DSS interceded and I did not have to go back with my mother. Instead, the social worker advised my mother to allow me to stay with my grandmother while they conducted an investigation. I did not admit anything to the caseworker, I was petrified but my grandmother spoke for me. She told DSS and the school officials that my mother had a serious problem, and they needed to do something before she killed me.

Finally, some relief, my grandmother had spoken up. I believe my plan to commit suicide scared her so much she had no choice. She loved her eldest granddaughter. More importantly, I know it is because God has a plan for me. Living with my grandmother was good, but I could not be rid of my mother forever. She was angry with my grandmother but eventually started coming back around. I ended up having to return to my mother. Things were not any better, instead of my mother using her fist; her verbal assaults became harsher. My grandmother made sure I visited with her often including the summers that made things a little better.

Life continued to be up and down for me with my mother even now, as I'm writing this book. God was in the midst of all that turmoil in my childhood. He holds the master blueprint of my life and my storyline continues to develop. I will become all that He destined for me to be.

CHAPTER NINE

The scars of my childhood impacted my life. I made poor decisions because I was desparate for something. There was a season in my life that does not make me proud. I'm happy Jesus looked beyond my fault and gave me what I needed. I'm grateful my past does not control my future. That is what I love about my Heavenly Father. He loves me unconditionally and my flaws doesn't count against me. He uses the person that does not have it all together.

Briefly, I dated a man who was seven years older than me. I got pregnant and had two children for him. I was a teenage mom. I thought my life was over but it was just the beginning. I thought the dreams I had were impossible to achieve now that I had broken my sacred covenant. Although I did not know God, I did not want to have sex outside of marriage.

He became my boyfriend because he was my "babysitter." What he told me was that for a quarter pound of reefer (marijuana), my mother said he could have me. (The devil thought he had a trap set for me). Drug and alcohol addictions can ruin a child's hopes and dreams when addictive parents make poor decisions for them. That is what my mother's decisions did to me. I did not have a choice but to believe him since I saw him give her and her boyfriend the huge bag of weed. They would leave me with him for hours at a time so they could have their "fun".

After several times of this happening I became his girl as he described. All I knew was I did not have a mother who loved me, rejected from birth, now sold to a man I didn't even like. He was a master manipulator of the circumstances of my life. Choices were made for me underhandedly and I succumbed, I was not strong enough to fight them. We stayed together for a little over five years until I got the strength to leave him. It was my nineteenth birthday. I have never looked back.

Beforehand, being under the power of my children's father and that relationship caused a great strain with my family. For the first time I felt what I was experiencing was true love. He reminded me how much it cost him to have me and I should love him. When you cannot recognize the authenticity of love, it is very easy to fall for the counterfeit forms of love and into trouble. I fell into that trap more than once. It took me years to be free from him.

I was a young woman with two babies but a drive and determination to have a better life for my children. I moved to my paternal grandparents' house on James Island. I went back to high school through an alternative program offered by my beloved James Island High School. I worked hard to earn my high school diploma. I was too smart to settle for a GED. I graduated a year behind my graduation class. My children deserved to have a better life than me. I needed to position myself to provide for them. I thank God for the support and love my aunts poured into my life. They accepted my children and went out of their way to help me raise and nurture them.

Living with my grandparents and very God-centered aunts made me curious about God. I began asking questions about faith and the reality of God. Why did they believe in God? Both of them have personal testimonies that gave me chills just listening to them speak. I enjoyed listening to my aunts and I tell others, my aunt have made me the woman I am today. I learned about the things of God from them. They showed me the way.

The curiosity about God's love for me kept me engaged in learning, and I felt a presence I cannot explain. Yes, I was a young woman who had sex out of wedlock and two beautiful children that were all mine, but my aunt said God loved me. Of course, I thought about the secrets I was hiding because I never told my father's side of the family the horrors I had faced as a child. I felt worthless and devalued so how could this perfect God care about me.

I asked my aunt about God and the meaning of salvation. We talked and she said the church was having a revival and she invited me to attend with her one of the nights. Monday night came and I did not go, I was still pondering, wrestling with "myself". Tuesday night she asked me again if I was ready, I told her no I did not feel like going. It was not until Thursday night that I went to church with her.

The prophet man preached on the power of the Holy Spirit; and how God sent that special gift so I would know I am never alone. That is what I wanted. Not to feel the emptiness I carried like a noose around my neck. Then the prophet began to list various hurts and sins we often committed but he said, "God loves you in your mess." He said, "God never used the perfect, the already got it together brother or sister, but the ones who were considered less-than in society."

The words that came out of his mouth truly touched my heart. His preaching compelled me. I felt I was coming alive as I sat there in the back of the very crowded church. As he ministered, I drifted off, not falling asleep but I saw pictures of my life. I was happy and whole. I saw myself strong and vibrant, oh how the tears welled up in my eyes. I thought to myself, "Lord if you are real please make yourself known to me that I may recognize you. I want what my aunts have in you."

The prophet opened the doors of the church and before he gave the appeal for non-Christians to come give their lives over to Christ, he said, "God has a special assignment for someone in this place tonight." I jumped up, ran down the aisle, and fell to the altar. I did not know why I reacted as quickly as I did, but something inside of me said; "Go", so I went. I knelt down not knowing how to pray so I wept and called on the Lord's name. The prophet came to me and said "young lady stand to your feet I have a message from the Lord for you." My aunt was standing by me, he said, "the Lord told me to tell you that He has much work for you to do and He will use you for His kingdom". These words I will never forget especially since God is now using me to share the Good News of Christ.

The prophet laid his hands on me and prayed. I felt something go through me that night unexplainable. I have come to know that a seed was implanted in me to be watered at the appointed time by my Father in heaven. He saved me and gave me a destiny all in one night.

On Sunday April 17, 1994, the pastor of the church baptized me. It was a joyous day for me, my two small children and my aunts were with me at the sunrise service to support and speak words of encouragement to keep on seeking the Lord.

CHAPTER TEN

I was saved and forgiven yet the feeling of freedom soon would leave me and the demons of my
past reappeared its ugly head. Saved but no power to
control my emotions and thoughts the enemy invad-
ed my mind with. I felt unworthy and unloved once
again. My aunt said, "You have to fight against those
thoughts, the enemy isn't going to leave you alone just
because you confessed Christ." She did not know I
was feeling that way because of the shame of having
my innocence taken and the physical abuse I suffered.
I studied the word of God every day. I prayed daily
and gave God my thoughts. Soon the struggle seemed
to be over, I was flourishing...or so I thought.

It was not until I was married and in my mid-twen-
ties that I would face the demons of my childhood

head on. I had not shared with my husband while we were dating the abuse I suffered as a child. Because of the shame, I could not reveal the sexual abuse to him. After I was healed, I shared with him my past so he would truly know his wife.

Before I received help, I was constantly depressed and oppressed. I needed help and needed it quick. My life was spiraling out of control and I once again felt suicidal. I was a struggling believer and I cried out to God for help. My thoughts beat me to a pulp every day. I did not deserve children, I did not deserve to be married, I was nothing, I was a fake Christian; the thoughts just went on nonstop. I spent hours crying.

Again, I asked God how can I be going through these things and call myself a Christian. I was going to church every Sunday, attended the bible studies during the week. I was active in church yet I had no power to defeat the enemy's fiery darts. I read the bible constantly and watched Christian television twenty-four hours a day. I knew my husband was angry but our television did not move from TBN. Once the suicidal thoughts was so burdensome, I sought professional help at a local counseling facility. After a brief discussion over the phone, the intake administrator told me to come right away. I was terrified if I could not get a whole on my thoughts my children would come home and find me dead.

God was making me a believer, I just did not know at that time my life would forever be changed. I arrived at the center, filled out paperwork, and had an intense therapy session.The counselor decided I should spend some time as an inpatient and I agreed. I was broken and did not know what else to do. My husband was shocked when I called to tell him I would be in the hospital for a few days and to please take care of the children. My counselor escorted me to a room and I sat on the bed. I was relieved that I was safe from myself. However, I was not at peace so I did as always I went into prayer. I watched the others who were hurting, some patients were yelling. I included them in my prayer. Although, I was not in a better state emotionally, my heart went out to them. My level of compassion grew and I began speaking to the Lord. I cried out to Him to please help me and help the others who were there with me.

I sat on the twin bed. There were no windows in the room and I prayed to God. I could not understand why bad things kept occurring in my life. I did what I believed was right. I worshipped daily, read my bible, prayed, lived in the church house and made sure I carried my children with me. I spent time listening for instruction. What was I doing wrong? Where was the power I always heard about? Why didn't I see the evidence of the Lord in my life? I had faith and believed in Jesus so what was I not doing not to have those things I often heard other people describe.

It was there in the quietness of that room that I heard the Lord talk to me "If you leave here I will heal you". At first, I thought I was out of mind and that I really needed to be locked away from the general population. After a while, I heard the Lord speak again, "If you leave this place I will heal you." Again, I said to myself "Hope stop talking to yourself, these people are going to think you are crazy if you go to them and tell them the Lord wants you out of this place."

A few more minutes went by, and I was in tears still praying and asking God to watch over my family while I was in the facility. I thanked Him for giving me the strength to drive myself there (in my suicidal state of mind). I had not told anyone I was going to admit myself to a mental facility. When I saw the commercial, I called the hotline and went there. Now I am hearing voices and do not know what I should do next.

As I sat at the edge of the bed I heard the voice of the Lord come to me again and say very firmly "if you leave this place I will heal you, trust in Me". It was at that exact time that the counselor that admitted me was walking by my door. I jumped up and called out to her, she stopped to ask me what was wrong. I told her that I had made a mistake and that I needed to get out this facility today.

At first, she said she could not release me because she felt I was a danger to myself. I told her I understood but that I needed to leave and I would not stop pushing the issue. I could not tell her that the Lord had spoken to me; she might have locked me up, and throw away the key. I could not let her think I was hallucinating. Instead, I trusted that if I kept pressing, the Lord would move on her heart and that is exactly what He did.

Finally, after she made me promise to see an outpatient psychiatrist and sign a no suicide risk waiver she released me. I left with an appointment but I did not keep it because God had done exactly what HE said he would do. He HEALED me. On the way home, I had never felt so free and alive. I had an assurance that I would be all right, it was then that my faith came into action.

After I got home, I held my children tight and told them how much I loved them. When my husband came home from work, I apologized for not being the best wife and that I loved him. I was overwhelmed with emotions and I thanked God for how He had blessed my life. I was caught up into what I did not have and had not paid attention to what I did have. I was saved through my confession of faith but had not been converted. I had not experienced real transformation in my life and soon my life changed for real.

God kept His promise and He took the brunt of the pain away from me instantaneously. He took away my guilt and shame. A few days later, I was watching a prominent television pastor as he ministered about being wounded and saved.

He spoke on how Christians do not deal with their childhood pain and many are not experiencing the true power of God in their life. He spoke these words right into my spirit man "God loves you and whom the Son has set free will be free indeed." Words so powerful, that it became one of my personal mission statement. I felt a shift within my soul and my life from that point would never be the same again.

I just remember crying throughout the entire broadcast, it was as if God was speaking directly to me. The message penetrated me so much I went from sitting on the couch to prostrating on the floor. I cannot really describe that moment in words but as I laid on the floor, I felt calm and warm all over my body. I was at total peace; if I was dying, I was ready because of what I experienced laying on my floor. I knew without any doubt that God was real and He truly loved me.

I spent what seemed to be an eternity on my living room floor talking and listening. For those of you, who will read this book and not understand what I am talking about, let me encourage you to try God for yourself. He has a way of revealing Himself to us. He is not a respecter of persons and wants you to know Him and make Him known to others. God poured His love into my life and I am forever changed.

It was because of my encounter with the Lord that I began the hard work; learning the power of love and forgiveness. You see, it was more important for me to forgive those that had hurt me. It took some time with God and sharing my wounded heart with Him, not once or twice but repeatedly until peace came. I had to breakdown the strongholds in my life but I could not do it apart from God. I had never been more real with God and I no longer had to hide because He knew all about me.

For the sake of Christ, I am an advocate for getting your love walk in order. Learn to forgive quickly for the reason of finding true freedom in your life. Even though people whom I should have trusted broke me, I had to love and forgive them. It was a slow and tedious process but I made it and I survived! I learned the purity of love and forgiveness by what Jesus did on the cross.

Jesus was spat on, beaten, and treated inhumanly by His own people. His closest friends, the disciples, abandoned Him. Yet from the old, rugged, shameful cross of Calvary, He prayed for His crucifiers, "Father forgive them for they know not what they are doing."

What Jesus did on the cross for a bunch of folks that did not deserve it, transformed me, and the way I think about love and forgiveness.

The word of God is so powerful especially in times of trouble, when the storms of life are raging. I was in bondage yet free, in trouble yet peace, sad yet joyful; I cannot articulate what I was going through any better. I was experiencing God differently as I became more spiritually disciplined and mature. The old Hope was steady dying as the new Hope was being born.

I spoke to other counselors and mentors that helped me to get through the rough days. God will place people in your life as you grow in grace to help you along the way. I am so grateful for the mighty men and women of God that walked me through my seasons, held my hand and gave me a shoulder to lean on when the burdens were too heavy to carry.

It was one year later the Lord called me into the ministry. It was not easy to accept the call because I still struggled with shame. I believed that to be in ministry I needed to be perfect. BUT GOD said not so, what the enemy had intended to stop my purpose He was going to use for good.

I had overcome so much but it was not for me. It was for whom God called me to minister too. The physical and sexual abuse I endured was for that woman or man who had been abused yet never felt the freedom to talk about it or share it with others.

It is because of my call into the ministry and having a pastor that was so transparent it forced me to acknowledge the events that happened to me. I had to confront my fear in order to be free. God knew what had happened, and allowed me to survive it, so now what? I looked at the bible differently because no one was perfect. God used many men and women mightily to speak his grace and perform on His behalf.

I was no different and I had to stop being a victim because I did not come from a flawless home, or had a textbook life. God wanted to use me anyhow, beyond my faults. He supplied all I needed. I am Hope, a woman whom God has carried through the storms of life. I was supposed to be strung out on drugs or an alcoholic-BUT LOOK At GOD. He has given me a destiny. I am not ashamed to tell the world who Jesus is because everybody ought to know whom Jesus is.

CHAPTER ELEVEN

I could write volumes if I wrote everything that happened to me as a child. I truly struggled writing this book. I had to confront the demons from my past. I started and stopped writing many times. It is not easy to be transparent in writing, at least it was not the case for me.

I am often asked where I get the strength to reveal so much of my life. No greater project have I felt the need to do for the Lord than write this book. My life became a roller coaster when I thought about the past but God reminded me it is not my present and my future will be even greater. He is a God of second chances.

Honestly, during the writing I went through phases of my faith, identity crises, and issues I thought I had conquered years ago resurfaced. I remember a very famous television pastor saying, "You can't conquer what you are not willing to confront." Nevertheless, I needed to write this book for my continued healing process. I focused on God and allowed him to lead me through the tough spots. I spent a lot of time worshipping and in prayer as I wrote; there was even a time I had to just stop writing and listen to His voice.

I remember hearing the Lord telling me that He had me and to keep my eyes on Him. God will speak in our distress and He has never let me down. God also spoke to me out of the book of John 8:36, "Whom the Son has set free is free indeed." I had lived in bondage for many years of my life and He assured me that I was free. Free from the persons that brought misery to my life; free to experience life as He always intended. This is how I will live for the rest of my life, FREE.

I no longer have to live with the wounds of my past. The wounds God healed will never hurt me again. I needed to let go and let God complete the work of healing that He had begun. It is not hard living as a Christian. It is hard living as a Christian when we feel powerless. I am so glad God's grace is sufficient to help us overcome the troubles of the world.

Thoughts of my family turning their backs on me, to people in the church shunning me, saturated my mind during the writing of this book. As I stated earlier, I was taught, "what happen in the family, stay in the family". Secrets can and have destroyed families. As I struggled, God reminded me that I was His child above my earthly family.

Jesus is at work inside of me and is faithful to complete his work because I am His handiwork. He molded and shaped me into the woman I have become. I decree these words over my life: I am stronger, better, and wiser. "I am more than a conqueror." I have learned, "the power of death and life" is in the power of my tongue. If I wanted to live and overcome, I had to keep speaking life. As long as I kept decreeing death, that was how I would live.

I can truly sing the old spiritual song "I'm Free" because I know the grace of God in my life. God taught me His love through my adversities. It is not where my story started but how well my story will end. God loves me unconditionally even in my struggle of fully accepting His love. "Let me say it again for those who may be dealing with guilt or shame, what I have learned is that God loves you unconditionally even in your struggle of fully accepting His love."

What I went through was not for me, but for all men, women, boys, and girls that will come across this book or hear my testimony and have assurance they can be free. He called me and He confirmed my purpose in life. Abuse imprisoned me for years, but I now live victorious. There are countless number of individuals dealing with the pain and shame of abuse. I can encourage and tell them God will give them peace that surpasses their own understanding. It is what the Lord did for me.

I waited on the Lord and He strengthened my heart to walk in love and forgiveness. I am not saying it was an easy journey, but God is faithful. He had heard my cries, seen my wounds, felt my pain and He healed me. I no longer have to walk around with my head hung low. I no longer have to travel with the past baggage on my back that weighed me down. The scripture instructed me to lay aside every weight and give all my burdens to Jesus so I can rest (refs. Heb 12:1 & Matt 11:28).

I am living in the rest of the Lord; this is not to say that I am problem free or still not have triggers that cause me to regress. I am equipped not to stay in that mindset. Practicing the spiritual disciplines of prayer, fasting, and studying God's word brings me to a place of peace during times I am battling the demons of my childhood.

I dealt with the emotional scars on the inside of me. God made a way for me to experience true joy and peace in my life. Securing a place of contentment was hard, but I'm enjoying where I am today. I can live free from the condemnation that kept me shackled to the memories of my past.

CHAPTER TWELVE

The truth of the matter is I did not know how this book was going to end. I prayed, "Lord please give me an unexpected ending." HE answered my prayer. I can shout from the rooftops, "Praise the Lord for He is good and His mercies endures forever (Psalm 100:5)."

I opened this book sharing the turmoil I experienced in my childhood. I was angry and unhappy for a significant part of my life. I should not have felt the pain of an emotionless parent, but I have come to understand some things since accepting Christ as my personal Savior.

It was not by chance but by purpose, the things I experienced. When I read the story of Job and others in the bible, I realize I have had an assignment since my birth. It did not catch God off guard when people

I trusted hurt me. They did not kill me. It did not catch Him off guard when I wanted to commit suicide. He is God and He knows everything. The scripture in Hebrews 13:8 teaches that Jesus Christ is "the same yesterday, today and will be forever."

He is the same God who saved Daniel from the lion's den, the three Hebrew boys from the fiery furnace, the nation of Israel from the hardships of Egyptian slavery. There are countless stories of God's deliverance of His children. He has no favorite children. He sees us all the same. God allowed me to go through some stuff, but make no mistake; He also carried me through it. He will do the same for each of His children.

There were times that I did not know Him or could not feel Him near me. Nevertheless, I now know God was there every step of the way. Yes, there were times when I was angry at God for allowing so much to happen to me, but it was all for His glory. He has given me opportunities to share my story in places I could not imagine. I have had countless women and men thank me for having the strength to share my testimony. I love seeing the intense look on the faces of the people I am ministering too. Not because they are so into me, but the idea they now know they too can be healed. They no longer have to keep shame as a part of their personal biography.

I had gone through the heartaches, frustration, and pain for this appointed time by God. I am living in the will of God striving each day to be the best Christian I can be through love, faith, and hope. Sometimes, I lift my head up gratefully to the skies and say, "thank you Lord for all you have done" and exhale.

My best days are still ahead of me. The enemy thought he had me, but I am so glad I have Jesus on my side. This book has been a refresher for me; it has allowed me to see God in an even greater way.

My aunts helped me state the correct facts of events. They reminded me, as did other relatives of the abuse they witnessed. My mother did not have any shame sometimes of where she reached out and smacked me.

I am so glad this book is ending with a destination of goodness. God could not have made it any better for me. His word is so true; He will give beauty for your ashes and turn your mourning into dancing. He will heal the broken hearted. He certainly did it for me.

I have always had a dream of hearing my mom just apologize for all the hurt and pain she caused in my life. One thing that I did not mention is that as I grew in grace with God; I also extended that grace to my mother and the man that hurt me. God's grace was sufficient for me and it would be for them because He is a forgiving God.

In 2011, I went to visit my grandmother's house for Mother's Day. I had not spent that holiday with my grandmother for a couple of years. Even though I had forgiven my mother I did not trust to be in the same place with her (fearful she would attack me). When I arrived, I noticed my aunts, grandmother, and mother sitting outside on the porch.

I did as always hug them but not my mother because she is not the touchy feely type. My two younger siblings were there so I walked into the house to greet them. As we were chatting, my mother came in the house and said she was happy to see her children there. Before I could move out of her way, she grabbed and hugged me. She said," Hopie, I love you and that's coming from the bottom of my heart." Naturally, I was tense and I was a bit skeptical.

I was shocked with what came next. My mother looking at my grandson and said to me, "Take care of your grandson and make sure your daughter takes care of him. Tell your daughter she does not want to be in my shoes. I'm sorry for all the pain I caused you." I said, "Momma I forgave you years ago." For years, what I had needed to hear finally came to fruition.

My mother even suggested us getting to know each other for the first time. It was at the time that my brother said, "Big Sis, momma has changed and you can take my word for it." In my heart, I pondered and said, "Lord thank you for the ending of my book." I left my grandmother's house on cloud nine, in expectation of the great things still yet to come.

A year has gone by and we try to stay in touch with one another. It is not perfect but at least I can talk with my mother now. The process has been slow, but God is still in the midst of our relationship. We will continue to build because I believe our latter days will be greater.

I am truly in a state of peace with my past. My wounds no longer hurt. My heart no longer aches. "I AM HOPE", purposed for this season to share the love of Christ and tell others they too can have freedom from a dark past.

Tearing down strongholds is what I am destined to do. I have learned the power of God's love and my passion is to share His love with the hurting world.

More From the Author...

Thank you for taking the time to read my story. I pray it has been a blessing to your life. Writing this book has not been without a challenge but nothing is when revelation is a part of the plan. I have many more stories of the abuse I suffered but revealing everything would have turned the book in a different direction.

Abuse is an evil that can destroy a person's soul. There are so many people hurting from wounds placed on them by physical, sexual and emotional abuse. Particularly in certain cultures, abuse is never to be spoken of. The family is not to be ashamed in anyway because we have an image to up keep. It does not matter if your poor eating pork and beans or wealthy eating prime rib steak, abuse is the secret that should go to the grave in some cultures. It is a crazy notion but it happens.

My personal opinion is that abusers do not know

or care about the pain they inflict. It is as if they separate truth from reality. I make the previous statement because I recall how bad I was hurting one day after his attempts to penetrate me. I had stayed in my room most of the day, not wanting to walk around for fear of anyone noticing me walking in a funny manner. I needed to go to the restroom and as soon as I walked into the hallway, he was there and said, "Hey, are you ok?" I looked up and shook my head, yes. In my mind, I was screaming, "you did this to me. I hate you for doing this to me." He went about his day as if he had not done anything to me. He walked right by with no apologies, he only seemed concerned because of the way I was walking and he thought he would be found out. I am so grateful God has delivered and healed me. All I have is the memories but the memories have no power over my life.

Today, I am a firm believer in God's word. I am blessed to be a blessing. I have people who have shared their testimonies and conquered the darkness of their past. I have many people who thank me for having the courage to speak about the forbidden secret. I do not know all God will have me to do. I cannot see my future but right now, He has empowered me to encourage, build up, and most of all LOVE.

I live by this motto, walk in love, extend grace, show mercy, forgive quickly and remain encouraged no matter what comes my way. I want to help others who are hurting. He has called me and I work every day to fulfill the calling on my life. My story has not ended; it is just beginning.

If you know of someone who is being abused, please call for help...

National Child Abuse Hotline
1-800-4-A-Chilld (422-4453)
National Domestic Violence Hotline
1-800-799-7233 or 1-800-548-2722
Healing Woman Foundation (Abuse)
1-800-477-4111
Visit the Following Websites for More Information
www.darkness2light.org

Hope,

First, let me say thank you so very much for trusting me with sharing your thoughts. I am honored you wanted me to read your book. I absolutely love you and this book. I knew when you posted the title of this book that I was going to read something special. Thank you for sharing, for encouraging and for being courageous!

Love you!
LaToya Williams